I0474499

# FOWL WISDOM

Identifying the Turkeys and Eagles in Your
Organization and Your Life

Jan Seahorn

iUniverse, Inc.
New York   Bloomington

# FOWL WISDOM

## Identifying the Turkeys and Eagles in Your Organization and Your Life

iUniverse books may be ordered through booksellers or by contacting:

iUniverse
1663 Liberty Drive
Bloomington, IN 47403
www.iuniverse.com
1-800-Authors (1-800-288-4677)

Because of the dynamic nature of the Internet, any Web
addresses or links contained in this book may have changed
since publication and may no longer be valid. The views
expressed in this work are solely those of the author and do
not necessarily reflect the views of the publisher, and the
publisher hereby disclaims any responsibility for them.

ISBN: 978-0-595-43230-1 (pbk)
ISBN: 978-0-595-87571-9 (ebk)

Printed in the United States of America

iUniverse rev. date: 10/14/08

To my sons and husband who taught me the greatest lessons about developing and valuing the importance of healthy, loving, and solid relationships. Life would be an empty journey without your love and support. My deepest gratitude and thanks.

Also, my sincere thanks to all of the organizations, students, and individuals with whom I have had the privilege to work and learn throughout my career. You have taught me more than any book I have ever read or workshop I will ever attend.

# Contents

# Note

In this book, I use eagles and turkeys to denote human stereotypes, realizing that both birds have their positive and negative characteristics. Benjamin Franklin, in fact, wanted the *wild* turkey to be the national bird. Personally, I am thankful that someone saw a more majestic model in the eagle. To be more specific, the text refers to the *barnyard* species of turkey versus the *wild*, country-roaming breed. Barnyard turkeys aren't nearly as resourceful as their undomesticated, wild cousins and tend to prefer less complex environments in which to live and toil.

# Preface

For the many people who are trying to be more productive, spend less time on ineffective meetings, engage in fewer stressful relationships, and live in healthier environments, *Fowl Wisdom* may give some insight into personal and professional behaviors that impact healthy systems. It may further readers' understanding of the conduct of those with whom they work and live in professional, social, and family environments.

The book offers information on communication, creating purpose versus busywork, and the difference between working with and being an eagle or a barnyard turkey. The turkey and eagle are characters who illustrate the importance of how human dynamics impact the productivity and well-being of any system.

Most organizations and individuals within these systems strive in various ways to serve others. Each of us has tremendous capacity to contribute our unique talents and gifts to the group's mission. It is when we forget our purpose or higher mission that we lose the vision of possibilities and the hope of achieving the mission's objective.

When we become ego-entrenched and see events only from a narrow "what's in it for me" perspective, there is no soaring like eagles. There are no limitless landscapes of possibilities. Hope and potential are replaced with discontentment and frustration. How easily we take on the behaviors of turkeys, strutting, gobbling, and complaining when things don't go our way, or when we forget that we are part of a larger social network that is influenced by the behaviors of everyone in the organization or family.

# Introduction

Change is exciting, annoying, invigorating, challenging, and, in many instances, intensely personal. It impacts our behaviors, our ideas, our emotional stability, and our precious status quo. We actively initiate some personal changes, such as going back to school, accepting a new job, buying a home, or choosing a mate. Even when we opt to make the change, it still has an emotional price tag attached. When change is not optional and is forced on us, the road can be even more difficult. It can be cognitively taxing and psychologically overwhelming. How we move through the change process is impacted not only by who we are as individuals, but also by whom we associate with as friends, family, and coworkers.

Watching others experience change, and having endured my own adjustments, I sometimes felt I was living in a barnyard of turkeys and at other times in a world of eagles. The turkeys were incredibly noisy and messy and somewhat scatterbrained—and at times I was one of the foul birds. When working with turkeys, the structure and leadership in the organization contributed to such polluted behavior. When missions were clear and meaningful and leadership robust, even turkeys had a chance to become more like eagles. These were also times when the true eagles in the group rose to their greater potential. In each case I was learning the "fowl wisdom" that each bird had to offer.

In our daily lives, most of us play the role of eagle and turkey, leader and follower. The wisdom spawned from each position enables us to be more fully human and humane as we allow ourselves to be humbled by our limitations and strengthened by our talents.

Thus, *Fowl Wisdom* is a metaphor for personal and organizational change and the human characteristics needed to make the journey successful. By "successful," I merely mean that we leave an experience with a greater sense of who we are, what we stand for, and how we hope to live the future. In other words, we've grown a bit of wisdom, even when the lesson was crushingly difficult or amazingly uplifting.

I deliberately chose the barnyard turkey and eagle as my main personas since one is more comfortable on the ground while the other seeks out the company of the wind and clouds. Both have their places, their talents, and their challenges.

I hope the format and the somewhat amusing style will engage the reader in reflective thought. Fowl/foul behavior is far too often displayed in board rooms, classrooms, and even in family rooms; and fowl/foul behavior casts doubt on the integrity and intention of the participants.

At first, I suggested that my black Labrador retriever, Chase, author this provocative literary piece. He is a master of bird conduct, but he alleged that he was too busy to contribute to this manuscript. Given that most bird dogs are not turkey hunters, I suspect that Chase's background knowledge is a bit limited in the area of turkeys and organizational change. Since I have a PhD in human development and organizational systems and over thirty years of experience working with numerous groups, it is certainly more reasonable that I create the manuscript.

I've internalized my experiences in various systems by wearing the shoes of a participant. I've spent countless hours listening as well-paid consultants tried to work miracles by attempting to guide dysfunctional groups down the yellow brick road to becoming a functioning team. At other times, I was that consultant—only not so well paid.

Currently I teach university courses on neuroscience, learning, and systems analysis. Even in the classroom there are similarities and differences in my students' ability to act competently. Some are eager, attend class regularly, keep up with assignments, and search to make connections with previous experiences. Others are much less proficient and responsible in taking ownership for their learning. The latter students are more comfortable in the memorize-test-dump system than the think-examine-question-and-apply-information process.

Yet, experience has taught me that the number one commonality of every group is that you can't change people or organizations that absolutely don't want to change or be changed. In the classroom, you can't force someone to learn unless and until he or she sees the value in being taught, in learning, and in mastering particular content. This is somewhat like forcing young children to eat oysters and hoping that somehow they will love the slimy creatures as they slide down their throat.

Yes, a group or individual may voice the need for change or the need to gain greater knowledge. But don't confuse "desire" with "determination." When you get right down to the hard work of changing, if change is to actually occur, members of the team must be willing, able, and sufficiently motivated to make the adjustments essential to bringing about that change.

Some groups are far more emotionally secure and more productive than others. Many I've worked with have behaved like eagles, soaring above adversity and maintaining a broad view of their landscape, while others have definitely been in the barnyard turkey category.

Eagles tend to be big thinkers, comfortable at taking risks and seeing their surroundings from various viewpoints. Turkeys can fly, but not very far, and they tend to do so only under extreme stress or in order to escape a predator.

Many of us have been in those "stay alive" situations, whether physical or emotional. You know the kind: the situations in which only an external, major threat has power to get us to move our butts in a different direction. It isn't that change under extreme stress is so terrible; it's just that waiting for a situation to become intolerable before we begin to change is emotionally draining and often physically and financially costly.

Even eagles get into stressful situations. Neither species is perfect; each has its own set of behaviors and strengths, as well as its limitations. It is the rare organization, family system, or even individual who always behaves like an eagle or a turkey. Most of us find ourselves somewhere on a continuum.

Within this range of functioning, we pose the question, "In our organization or family, are we, for the most part, behaving like and attracting eagles, or are we, more often than not, functioning at the level of barnyard turkeys?" Responding honestly to this query will offer the questioner an opportunity to explore and find out whether, given the personal and professional characteristics of the group, productive change is even a possibility.

Using the fowl metaphor, I ask the reader to explore and analyze the actions of his or her own team. The task is to create a body of evidence that focuses on reasons for celebration and that provides opportunities to engage in constructive conversations on ways to improve.

Self and group reflection are essential. If an organization makes time for discussion, analysis, and assessment of current work environments, dynamic change may take place. Without reflection, meaningful change may be impossible. Spotlighting the positives, such as what has worked, how far the team has come in meeting its goals, and honoring the culture of growth, stimulates enthusiasm. Remembering and celebrating small successes offers the critical lifting power necessary for both eagles and turkeys to fly.

Frankly, fowl/foul behavior has taught me a great deal about patience, trust, persistence, developing strong bonds and relationships, and maintaining them. Living and working with others is not a static venture. These bonds and relationships are always shifting towards well-being or disorder. Folks who think environments and relationships are stable are fooling themselves. Social interactions, whether at home, at work, or in a community, build health and productivity or crumble toward the compost pile.

Creating and maintaining healthy social and emotional relationships is an individual's and an organization's real work. Both turkeys and eagles need environments that allow them to feel physically and emotionally safe. They need nourishment to thrive, and they need role models that show them the possibilities for fulfilling their enormous potential. Creating relationships isn't about creating "Kumbaya" moments; it is about how our brains are set up for survival— survival that involves trust, safety, and being with a community of others.

So what makes us act like turkeys or soar like eagles? Read on to discover your true fowl identity.

# Chapter 1

# Readiness and Change

What a mess! What a shame. How utterly sad. I left the day's session frustrated, angry, depressed, and wondering what the heck I was doing. As a consultant, I was supposed to be leading this company, Zero-org, through a dynamic reconsolidation of its system and helping the leadership team identify strengths and concerns that the change process was definitely going to bring to light.

Before accepting the assignment, I had talked extensively with the administration regarding the current state of the organization as well as about the ability of the company's leadership team to lead. I wanted to be confident that the group was aware of the change that was to take place. I was hoping that the organization had a well-established, high-functioning leadership team with a track record for being successful within the workplace.

The CEO assured me that Zero-org was ready and eager to proceed. The administrators proudly stated that their team had been carefully chosen to represent the various stakeholders within the organization and that each individual was a competent leader in his or her own role.

Nothing could have been further from reality. Not only was this organization not the least bit ready for change, but until I chaired the first meeting, their "leadership team" never even *existed*. To make matters even more interesting, the members of the team had no idea why they were at that meeting or what they were to be doing, and most of the members had no *desire* to lead! They did, however, say they loved the refreshments that we provided during the session. Fat, sugar, and carbs seem to really appease a clueless group.

This "oh my God" moment was my first piece of evidence that the change journey with Zero-org was going to be a nightmare.

## "Oh My God," Moment Number One

*Never take administration or anyone else at their word without going in to observe firsthand the culture, climate, and overall environment of the organization. It isn't as though the leaders intentionally misled me about their status. I'd like to think it was more a discrepancy in our definitions of* ready *and* leadership. *What I considered high functioning and capable seemed to be quite different from their interpretations of the words. By the end of the initial meeting, I was beginning to hear the sound of gobble, gobble, gobble.*

# Chapter 2

# Evidence of a Leadership Turkey Brigade: "The Land of Nothingness"

By now, you might be asking, "What's the problem? If the leadership team was so inept, why not just teach them how to be better leaders? Give them a role model and act like a leader. Show them; then they will *do*."

Wonderful! Simple! But after several weeks, reality set in, and I realized that inspiration, aptitude, understanding, and the feeling that the change would be valuable weren't among the group's traits. This was my second *"Oh my God,"* moment.

## "Oh My God" Moment Number Two

*You can't make lemonade out of potatoes. Even Michelangelo knew that he had to have material that would hold up to the sculpting, pounding, and forming required in creating the statue* David, *I knew what I needed, and I knew that this team may not be able to hold up under the intense pressure of change. They would definitely need additional support, structure, time, and information to develop into an effective team.*

One of the leadership team's and administration's problems was obvious: they never achieved desired outcomes. When they did get something done, they didn't do it in the manner that they agreed upon during our meetings. There was no momentum to move forward.

For example, when the team approved a particular course of action with specific measures and a clear timeline, several weeks later when we held the next meeting, *nothing* had been accomplished. There was always an excuse— lack of time, someone thought someone else was going to do it, or they got busy and forgot. Gobble, gobble, gobble.

It was clear that neither the leadership team nor the administration was willing to take ownership for its own change process. Perhaps they felt that simply attending meetings and talking about the change would be enough to make change happen. Gobbling isn't the same as taking action.

Another problem was their organizational messages. Since few people beyond management had anything to do with gathering essential information regarding the change and communicating it to others, *nothing* seemed to make sense to the people who were expected to accept and implement the mandated modifications. No one had informed them why a change needed to be made. This only increased the gobbling and complaining.

It seemed that the leadership team never quite knew where they were going or why they were going there. They suggested that they had never had a clearly identified purpose in the first place, and that what purpose they had was not one they agreed with and wanted to pursue.

As a consultant, my task was to help with the change process. Zero-org's responsibility was to fully participate in identifying, accepting, and conveying a clear vision of change that would benefit the company, its employees, and the stakeholders whom the company served.

Instead, the identified course kept changing direction. The harder the team tried to focus, the more obscure the course became. Though the goals became clearly defined, the team wasn't implementing them. Even when they tried to regain focus, they seemed to veer off course. They were stagnating in the *Land of Nothingness.*

## Leadership Problems in the Land of Nothingness

When I examined some of the obstacles the organization had faced over the previous years, what I found was disturbing and revealing. The organization had five different CEOs in seven years and two different managers in three years, each with his or her own agenda and way of doing things. Employees left for better job opportunities, saw the dysfunction and jumped ship after a year, or were fired for ineffectiveness.

Many of the new executives wanted to lead by a top-down management style—the kind of style in which managers made all of the decisions, told employees what to do, and then expected them to do it. Under that approach, employees didn't have to worry about going to many meetings, making decisions, or working as a team. They merely had to follow orders without questioning or thinking. Unfortunately, many in the organization had become quite comfortable with this model of leadership – follow the leader blindly without asking where we are going or why.

Then there was the manager who was collaborative to the point that few decisions ever were made, actions were rarely carried out, and no one knew who would do the work. Given the fact that the management team had never been trained in collaboration and that most employees were relatively satisfied with the "follow the leader" type of management, teamwork was a foreign concept.

To make matters worse, there never seemed to be enough time for groups or individuals to meet and establish common understandings, practices, or to develop new skills or procedures. Little to no effort was being spent building those healthy relationships that are the crucial glue that bonds organizations together for the tough journeys ahead.

The culture was going through incredible change, and the organization's leaders had not placed enough emphasis on team building, expectations, "meaning making," or professional interactions. No wonder they were in the Land of Nothingness.

In the end, all the work and progress the team made after several years of grueling effort went down the tubes when yet another new CEO came on board and decided that he wanted to implement his own agenda. Once again, Zero-org's team members were thrown into the world of "change the change" before the organization had the opportunity to solidify its progress and sustain what it had initially started.

## Lessons from the Land of Nothingness

Yep, change was certainly something these employees could trust. They could trust that change probably would never happen because the top level of the company seemed unstable and unable or unwilling to commit to a sustainable leadership model. Leadership teams could trust that they would not receive the resources necessary to carry out their mission. And they could expect that this new CEO would leave after a few short years only to be replaced by an individual with yet another agenda.

Turmoil like this doesn't develop healthy relationships or confidence. Change is difficult enough when people trust and respect one another. When they don't, coalitions form that draw everyone into battle. The change becomes more about individual agendas than about achieving the group's or organization's mission. People lose sight of the big picture and spend enormous amounts of time on small, insignificant details.

Establishing and maintaining a solid sense of direction is nearly impossible in such a chaotic environment. If leaders want to stay out of the Land of Nothingness, they will need to create a clear vision for the change and be strong enough to enforce and monitor an explicit course of action. Just as important, leaders will need to be thoughtful and vigilant about defining what change is absolutely necessary for their organization to succeed and give adequate time, money, training, and additional resources to implement the change and carry it through until it is sustainable. If leaders can't do this, then it is better to not waste people's precious time, minds, and hearts.

## To Think and Talk About

*It is easier to work with people you have developed a sense of trust and hope with and who have an identifiable, clear, and creditable mission—people you believe have the strength and integrity of eagles, and people who will be around long enough to see the change through from beginning to end.*

Organizations and families that are capable of making change happen without pecking each other to death establish a meaningful sense of purpose and hold each other accountable for personal actions and responsibilities. They believe each member of the team to be trustworthy as well as trusting. They recognize that each person has the potential to be an eagle, a leader, and a responsible supporter of the mission. Leaders share ownership for the well-being of their organization and the people in it. They are willing and able to devote the necessary financial and emotional resources both financial and emotional needed to accomplish the mission.

## Leaders ask and constantly monitor the following:

- **What have we and our organization done to build healthy relationships?**

- **What still needs to be done?**

- **Do we have enough eagles to accomplish your mission?**

- **How can we develop more eagles in your organization?**

- How do we or could we invite and encourage turkeys in our organization to become eagles?

- Do we have the resources we need to engage in this change? If not, where can we access these resources?

- Is the organization willing to devote the necessary time and direction to make the change truly sustainable?

# Chapter 3

# Turkeys vs. Eagles

By now you may be trying to determine whether your organization has created healthy, productive relationships or is struggling to overcome unhealthy adversity. Healthy groups need teams of eagles if they are to be successful, and they need (undomesticated) turkeys that are intelligent supporters.

You also may be attempting to determine which group you have in your barnyard and asking who are the turkeys and eagles. Or you may assume that you already know. Be careful of your classification process, however, because what you think you know, you may not know, and those you point fingers at often point right back at you!

There may be eagles among you that look like turkeys because their wings have been clipped and their spirits battered. In the same manner, there may be turkeys that look like and mimic eagles but in reality aren't capable of flight and wouldn't have the slightest concept of how to see the big picture even if God himself gave it to them.

## Turkeys and Eagles

In our work and family lives, each of us will, at times, need to be the undomesticated turkey who wants to follow the guidance of another, but we must follow with intelligence and insight rather than with blind trust. Even in the turkey family there are those who, when provided the appropriate resources and dynamic environments, can be leaders and complex-problem solvers. So if you can identify the turkeys in your barnyard, you will be able to help each of them occasionally be eagles. They will be a whole lot happier if they are able to soar. now and again.

*Nevertheless, eagles have assets that turkeys don't have. They are better sighted and not afraid of journeys that require leaving the ground. They are risk takers, yet they are generally not foolish in their ventures. They would rather live in daring surroundings with complex challenges than scratch on the ground with narrow views of their environment.*

Most *domesticated* turkeys, on the other hand, aren't the neatest of the bird species. They are not built for flight, and they have limited vision. Although they can manage liftoff for very short distances, they tend to be peckers and perchers. They prefer to rely on what is already on the ground for a meal than spend time and energy pursuing more active food sources.

At Zero-org, the eagles were getting pecked to death by their unhealthy turkey peers. Every time a team member tried to be creative or look at possibilities that could move the organization forward, some team members did their best to nibble them to death.

Other leadership team members at Zero-org wanted to maintain the status quo at all costs. Many of them did not *want* to fly; they were quite content being securely tethered to the old way of doing things. After all, taking on new ideas and procedures meant change, and change meant work. Work meant time and greater effort. Therefore, change was to be avoided, stomped on, and buried beneath foul behavior.

This was my third *"Oh, my God"* moment.

## "Oh My God" Moment Number Three

*I realized that the eagles on the leadership team couldn't survive the attacks of so many unhealthy turkeys. The closer we came to implementing an action, the more feathers the eagles lost. They were beginning to look like birds that were undergoing chemotherapy.*

Your organization may have several members that mimic turkey behavior. Risk taking seems somewhat formidable to them, and these barnyard fowl seem quite content to stay with the status quo or refer back to the good old days. Change of any kind is unsettling. Some individuals, like the barnyard turkey, are conditioned to taking orders and carrying out responsibilities that have been clearly defined in microscopic detail. Thinking autonomously seems not to be within their comfort zones.

Such inert behavior may have been valued in the past and, in some organizations, even nurtured. Today's workplace, however, requires very different skills and attitudes to survive. It demands and depends on flexible, responsive, and creative problem solvers. These are the traits of eagles and risk-taking turkeys who try to fly because they begin to enjoy the freedom and exhilaration of the journey.

In contrast, passive turkeys are generally followers, not leaders. They aren't very adaptable, curious, or self-sufficient. They need to be fed because they won't forage for their food, and they loved to gobble, gobble, gobble.

Organizations will always require some of their workers to be followers on occasion. The difference in today's work environment is that even followers need to be adaptive because they will have to lead when the opportunity or situation presents itself. It is this delicate balance between leader and follower that keeps an organization, a family, or a community dynamic and successful.

Consulting with a variety of systems, I have found numerous individuals who appear to be working hard to be eagles. The biggest problem with some systems lies in their workers' inability to toil as an efficient team: both eagles and healthy turkeys working toward a common goal. There are too many coalitions vying for power. Many individuals have lost sight of the organization's purpose and mission. They have become myopic, successfully having their short-term needs met at the expense of long-term goals. There is very little *giving* and a great deal more *taking*. Even eagles can be part of the problem if they aren't willing to be part of the team. No system, whether it is a family or a large corporation, prospers in such selfish surroundings.

Human beings are social organisms. Our survival depends on cooperation and interconnectedness. The more complex the problem, the greater the need for many people who can solve the problem through genuine collaboration and the full utilization of human resources. Solving problems has never been "one for one"; it has always been "one for all." Anything less challenges our humanity and exchanges our humility for arrogance.

Valuing, respecting, and honoring individual strengths and differences support healthy relationships. Every member of a team or family must be expected to contribute productively to a group's mission and goals. And every member must be given the opportunity to contribute his or her talents. When opportunity to contribute is stifled and human capabilities are thwarted, potential is lost.

## To Think and Talk About

*Every person in an organization should strive to develop a capacity to be both an eagle that soars and an (undomesticated) turkey that is intelligent and thoughtful. Healthy eagles and turkeys enjoy moving beyond their normal environment to enjoy new and exciting landscapes.*

One of my favorite examples of a healthy workplace and leadership team came when I was working with a staff of educators undergoing enormous changes in administration, school structure, and student population. Every response to a challenge the team faced was always focused on what was best for students, not what was easiest for the faculty to implement. The vast majority of the leadership team was comprised of eagles who, when they needed to, would become productive turkeys. These individuals were incredibly willing to see issues from the perspective of others and weigh the merits of each idea according to feasibility and value. Members of this team were able to solve extremely complex problems and take their entire school staff and its students to more meaningful learning environments and student achievement.

## Questions for Leaders and Teams to Consider:

- Which are you: A healthy eagle? A productive (undomesticated) turkey? An egotistical eagle? An unhealthy, inert turkey?

- Which of these are your teammates and co-workers?

- What evidence do you have that supports your assumptions about yourself and your co-workers?

## Fowl Talk and Behavior:
## A Guide for Human Behavior

### Barnyard Turkeys

### Eagles

| | |
|---|---|
| ➤ Peck and gather only what is immediately available | ➤ Make discrete organizational choices and look for options |
| ➤ Depend on what is currently in supply and can't or won't go very far to find it | ➤ Can choose from a variety of resources and are willing to go great distances to find additional resources |
| ➤ Tend toward foul behavior (i.e., complaining, whining, gossiping, gobbling) | ➤ Tend to engage in positive behaviors (i.e., proactive thinking, reflecting, and acting) |
| ➤ Create only short-term or easily attainable goals—attitudes, behaviors, skills, knowledge not developed for success | ➤ Generate both short- and long-term goals—minds, attitudes, skills developed for soaring. Monitor all goals and actions |
| ➤ Are noisy critters— "Gobble, gobble" | ➤ Quiet creatures—good at listening Patient—willing to wait longer to have needs met |

➤ Are impatient—like to have needs met immediately

➤ Believe only in what they can see immediately in front of them—shortsighted

➤ Go with the group mentality

➤ Believe only in what has already been done—easily discouraged

➤ Accept what is, but are anxious of thoughts of what can be.

➤ Believe in possibilities and hopes—see great distances with accuracy and optimism

➤ Easily follow and imprint on others

➤ Free spirited. Carefully guide others, but are willing to be thoughtfully led

➤ Imprint on others? You've got to be kidding!

➤ Don't believe in impossibilities—have can do determination and persistence

➤ Challenge what is to become what can be—work hard to achieve difficult goals fueled by significant missions.

- Where are you on the preceding list?

- Where are your peers?

- Where is your organization?

- How do you know this is true?

- What can you do to become more like eagles?

- What are you willing to do to become more like eagles?

# Chapter 4

# Communication: Gobble, Gobble

Leaders beware! Groups who are sloshing in a barnyard of slime that is toxic and stinky need to look at the topic of communication and leadership.

Toxic environments don't get that way by happenstance. One variable that contributes to toxicity is dishonest or unclear communication within the organization. Some authors of organizational development materials insist on the importance of "crap detecting," or discovering what parts of the group's communication are honest and genuine. So do some crap detecting by asking yourself this question: what parts of the messages in my group are fabrications, deceptions, or illusions perpetrated to instill apprehension? Healthy workplaces inspire a sense of honesty, trust, and hope through clear messages that consistently communicate the group's mission and purpose for existing.

Leadership is crucial in delivering both the hope and the consistency of the message, yet every person in the organization is responsible for acting on the message in ways that contribute to the organization's success. The words may change, the actions may be adjusted, but the message remains the same. Successful communication rests on clarity and wholeness. It requires a message that brings with it a sense of significance, a sense that the work people do can and will make a difference for the organization and its stakeholders.

Healthy workplaces encourage open dialogue about the processes and strategies that move them toward achieving their goals and dreams. Leaders must allot ample time and opportunity for such dialogue so the strategies can move toward achieving the organization's objectives. Meaning is inferred only when groups have sufficient time with each other to develop a sense of duty and personal responsibility.

One of the most common barriers to good dialogue is lack of time. Yet when leaders place a high value on building teams and achieving the mission, they can find enough of this elusive rogue—time.

One successful system found time by eliminating unproductive staff meetings and delivering updates and reports through e-mails, memos, and bulletin boards. Meetings could then be dedicated to learning new strategies and skills and discussing what was working, not working, or in need of adjustment. They were then able to address problems in a judicious manner, analyze data for patterns and evidence that objectives were being met, and evaluate strategies for effectiveness.

Such constant and rigorous communication enabled the organization to meet all of its yearly goals ahead of its projected schedule.

## Accountability

Additionally, healthy workplaces hold people accountable for maintaining high standards of behavior and ethics. On numerous occasions, It's common to hear of groups who speak the words but don't walk the walk. Informal meetings occurred in staff parking lots, cafeterias, and lounges where the discussion was a whining session about who wasn't doing what. Individuals groaned about the managers, principals, or leaders who weren't holding people in the organization to agreed-upon expectations. Gobble, gobble. Peck, peck. Blame, blame.

Few of these complainers ever took responsibility for confronting their peers for inappropriate behavior. It was easier to grumble than to be proactive and address the situation. Yep; like gobbling turkeys, they would rather peck, nitpick, and ramble than behave with the strength of an eagle and confront their peers responsibly and appropriately.

Too few individuals recognize or accept the fact that accountability is the responsibility of every person in the system—each worker, each leader, or each family member. Every member of any type of team must hold others, and himself, liable for achieving the mission. Therefore, every person needs to be both an eagle that strives to see the bigger landscape and a healthy turkey that supports the team's work in accomplishing the goal.

I know of few organizations whose personnel and leaders do not work hard. More often, however, I have seen groups in which the real work is sporadic, the initiatives poorly implemented, and the mission or goal fuzzy and vaguely defined. No wonder chaos abounds. No one is quite sure where the barnyard is heading, why it is heading there, and how it will get there safely.

Toxic, ambiguous communications and inconsistent accountability damage relationships, stifle organizational and individual growth, and make desired change difficult, if not impossible, to achieve.

### To Think and Talk About

*Eagles don't talk much, yet when they do, their messages are clear, focused, and motivating. Turkeys do a great deal of gobbling, pecking, and complaining without saying much.*

- How and how often does our organization communicate?

- Does the communication promote health or toxicity in our people? Give examples.

- Does our organization's communication inspire hope, clarity of purpose, and positive relationships? Give examples.

- Does the communication support the attainment of goals that align with a purposeful mission? Give example.

- Are the goals, programs, and actions monitored and adjusted regularly to assure that what is being done is making a difference? Give examples.

- Do these results get communicated in a timely and effective manner to the entire organization? When? How? Who delivers the information?

- Does every individual take responsibility for upholding the standards of the group? Give examples.

# Chapter 5
# Purpose or Busywork

Back in the eighties and early nineties, organizations spent an incredible amount of time and money to dialogue, brainstorm, and develop mission statements. Maybe yours was one of these groups. I only wish I had a small fraction of the wealth many consultants made taking people through these time-consuming exercises. It wasn't that the dialogue wasn't worthwhile or the mission statements weakly written. Okay, it's true: some of them were dreadful and a lamentable waste of time.

A major problem with mission statements was that most were far too long, and few people ever seemed to actually know, much less understand, what the proclamation meant, even if the company went to great lengths to put it on huge, colorful banners plastered all over the walls.

Rarely did the group ask as it went through the process, "What is our work?" "What do we *fundamentally* stand for?" "How do we make a difference by doing what we do?" In other words, they hardly ever asked, "What is our main purpose for existing?"

Every once in a while, a group created a mission statement that was functional. So let's pretend that yours was one of the organizations that crafted a decent mission statement. Did everyone in the organization (including the CEO) know what it was? Did anyone ever use it? How? When? Did *anyone* care?

Maybe after spending enormous amounts of resources on their mission statements, organizations tired of wasting time and money creating them are now starting to actually use them. In order to be effective, a mission statement must be well structured and concise. Few turkeys *or* eagles have enough brain space to remember long, drawn-out, wordy declarations. I'm always posing the question, "If your mission statement is more than one sentence long (and more than twenty words), which part of it isn't important enough for people to remember?" Usually, I get that "deer in the headlights" or "you're fired" look from the top executive.

The main reason a group needs a strong mission statement is to actually plan on living it. By *plan* and *living it*, I mean that every action, every resource, including time, money, people, and organizational structure, will be dedicated to achieving the mission. For example, if you were an educational institution, your mission statement might sound something like this:

> We strive to provide challenging, diverse, and neuroscience-based (brain-compatible), appropriate learning experiences to all children, supporting success and achievement now and in the future.

Curriculum content, professional development, and training would all reflect the organization's actions and efforts to accomplish the mission. Money for new programs or staff positions would align with the structure and environment of the system to maximize human efforts and abilities. The question, "How will this make a constructive difference for *all* students?" would continually be posed.

There would be no statements such as "for *most* or *some* students"; all means *all*, and every effort would be made to live that mission. Educators would know it, parents would know it, and most of all, students would know it, and all would be held accountable for living it!

## What prevents an organization from achieving its mission statement?

1. You have a useless mission statement—one that's
   - Too long,
   - Not specific or clear, or
   - Filled with big, flowery words with no substance.
2. No one knows what the statement is.
3. No one cares what the statement is.
4. No one uses the statement, or only a few use it.
5. No one is held accountable for living the statement.
6. Little time is spent on reflecting, discussing, and evaluating the meaning, value, and utility of the mission statement.
7. Progress toward living the mission statement is not documented, monitored, or openly celebrated.
8. The mission statement is not enduring or meaningful in its core. Every few years (sometimes every year), a new mission statement is written and the organization starts all over again.

Inert turkeys love pecking in barnyards with long, meaningless, unlived mission statements.

This makes it easier for them to gobble more and louder, peck at each other until they draw blood, and run around like chickens (*oops*—turkeys) with their heads cut off.

Eagles, like healthy people working in noxious environments, must get out of toxic barnyards as soon as possible. They must depart before they get their wings snipped, are gnawed to death, or are stuck in a messy, stinky, foul farm.

The worst of all scenarios, however, occurs when an eagle begins to lose sight of a truth or loses hope that he or she is an eagle and takes on the beliefs, behaviors, and expectations of the turkeys. When this happens, a valuable potential is destroyed, and the organization has lost the opportunity to cultivate and use the full talents of a present or future leader.

In toxic family and organizational cultures, eagles are frequently shattered by the helplessness and hopelessness of truly foul environments with meaningless missions and conflicting efforts. No society can afford such wastefulness. Organizations, families, and community groups must be relentless in implementing strategic measures to thwart the loss of its human gifts. The cost of not doing so will be far more than a society can afford to pay in intellectual, social, moral, and financial assets.

## To Think and Talk About

*A purpose that is meaningful makes sense and generates inspiration. Principle-guided actions enable an individual and give an organization the stamina to accept the challenges and to reflect on and learn from the journey.*

- **Does our organization have a strong sense of purpose? What is it?**


- **What is meaningful in our purpose?**


- **Who will profit by achieving our mission/ purpose?**


- **What would it take for us or our organization to develop this purpose?**

# Chapter 6

# There Will Always Be Barnyards

There will always be barnyards, some healthy, some noxious. It is far better to be living in organizations where attention is paid to the physical and emotional environments of the occupants. Noxious environments can be devastating. Smart eagles and turkeys will move out of unhealthy surroundings to keep their bodies, spirits, and souls intact.

Sometimes I hear people distressing over too much change, too many or not enough occupants in the barnyard, insufficient or poor resources, or inadequate leadership. They worry about the future rather than paying close attention to the present. They spend most of their efforts and time anxious about whether they will have the means, stamina, or spirit to sustain the change.

Wise people pay close attention to the present, understanding that what takes place today will impact the success of tomorrow. If the barnyard is well maintained today, it is likely to thrive in the future. These astute individuals know which situations are within their circle of control and which are not; that is, they understand which variables they can influence and which variables are too expensive or beyond their physical or emotional resources to manage.

The future depends on addressing concerns and obstacles directly. Denial expressed in such language as, "out of sight, out of mind," or "what will be, will be," is mentally irresponsible. Only in a passé song would one get by with such unsound thinking. In real life, you are going to be buried in endless mounds of muck unless you take some kind of thoughtful, effective action to address problems and move forward.

In our current world, there is no shortage of obstacles. Organizations that have done their work in building relationships, establishing effective communication systems, creating a strong sense of purpose, and preparing all members to be both eagles and healthy turkeys will be better prepared to navigate the challenges of change.

These prepared people are the eagles and the more adventurous undomesticated turkeys. They are brave enough, confident enough, tough enough to acknowledge and deal with what is real. These are the turkeys that can become eagles when they need to. Each is willing to embrace challenges, knowing that all winds are not calm, and that even the worst storms will eventually pass.

*It's not so much that we're afraid of change or so in love with the old ways, but it's that place in between we fear… It's like being between trapezes. It's Linus when his blanket is in the dryer. There's nothing to hold onto.*

—Marilyn Ferguson

*Man cannot discover new oceans unless he has courage to lose sight of the shore.*

—Andre Gide

## To Think and Talk About

*There will always be barnyards and, hopefully, they will be healthy, hearty, and filled with sturdy inhabitants who can gather the information and the knowledge required and develop the essential skills to keep the organization safe and thriving throughout the journey. Group members trust in their potential, build healthy relationships, and pay attention to their mission. They understand that the courageous live fully, while the timid merely suck oxygen and take up space.*

## Questions to Consider

- Which barnyard are we in now?

- What challenges are we currently addressing?

- What are we refusing to confront?

- Do we have the information, knowledge, and skills to be successful? Make a list of these.

- What are the strengths of our people?

- What are our areas of concern?

# Characteristics of High-Performing Teams

## They:

⇨ Practice effective interpersonal skills: genuinely listening, speaking, reflecting, and respecting and acknowledging others. These techniques keep the gobbling to a minimum.

⇨ Pay attention to developing group and interpersonal skills, not just completing the task at hand. High-performing teams know that people are every bit as important as the end product.

⇨ Increase trust, communication, and the ability to manage conflict through teaching, learning, and practicing personal and interpersonal skills.

⇨ Take action based on a well-designed, thoughtful plan; monitor the plan on regularly and make adjustments that enable the organization to move forward in a more productive manner; and collect a wide body of evidence that what they are doing is making a difference.

⇨ Always debrief meetings and hold discussions that reflect and evaluate the group's behavior, and remove any obstacles to productivity. These teams don't ignore the elephants in the room—they understand that the elephants will grow larger and the environment may become even more foul.

⇨ Make time for celebrations.

# Concerns and Solutions

1. What are the *biggest* problems or concerns our organization or family is currently facing? Are we surrounded by so much "stuff" that we can't begin to focus on the real problems?



2. What are some possible strategies and solutions/alternatives that we might use to help with our problems/concerns? In other words, how can we give our domesticated turkeys "a bird makeover"?

# Questions for Constructing a Team Action Plan

1. What do we like that our organization is already doing?

2. What should or can we add to enable it to do better?

3. How should we do this?

4. When should we do this?

5. How can we keep track of, evaluate, and document our progress?

6. How do we communicate our work and progress to others within our organization? To our stakeholders?

# Afterword

Even though Chase, my Labrador hunting retriever (please see picture in the Introduction), was not capable of being a part of this project, he is quite intrigued about future works. He recommends that I write about pheasants or maybe even rabbits next time. As a hunting dog, he knows more about this topic and is quite interested in any information on their living habits.

To the many men and women who love, raise, or hunt turkeys, I do hope that you haven't taken offense at what I've said in this book about your favorite fowl. Whatever you do, do not send me comments or complaints about your precious turkeys. I already have enough *###* *i*n my life and do not need any additional material to add to my compost pile.

Many thanks and genuine gratitude.


## PS

If you feel compelled to send comments to someone, please forward all sensitive information to your congressman. He or she has an entire staff highly trained to deal with CRAP and turkeys.

# About Janet J. Seahorn, PhD

Dr. Seahorn has been a teacher, administrator, and consultant for thirty years. She is currently an adjunct professor for Regis University in Denver, and Colorado State University in Fort Collins, Colorado, where she teaches several classes on neuroscience and literacy. Dr. Seahorn has a PhD in human development and organizational systems. She has an in-depth understanding of assessment, neuroscience research, and effective practices in organizational systems and change. Dr. Seahorn conducts numerous workshops on the neuroscience of learning and memory systems and the effects of at-risk environments (e.g., poverty) on brain development.

Dr. Seahorn has worked with many organizations in the business and educational communities in creating and sustaining healthy, dynamic environments. Currently, Dr. Seahorn and her husband are in the final publishing stage of a book on post-traumatic stress disorder for veterans and their families called *Tears of a Warrior: A family's story of combat and living with PTSD.* She has recently completed another book, *When Crap Happens, Grow Zucchini: How to live with dying and appreciate the crap.*

You may contact Dr. Seahorn at www.teampursuits.com or www.tearsofawarrior.com.